P9-DUB-066

BOA
EDITIONS
LIMITED

BELL 8

poems by

RICK LYON

FOREWORD BY C. K. WILLIAMS

BOA Editions, Ltd. ❧ Brockport, NY ❧ 1994

LC #: 94–70457
ISBN: 1–880238–08–x cloth
ISBN: 1–880238–09–8 paper

First Edition
94 95 96 97   7 6 5 4 3 2 1

The publication of books by BOA Editions, Ltd.,
is made possible with the assistance of grants from
the Literature Program of the New York State Council on the Arts
and the Literature Program of the National Endowment for the Arts,
as well as from the Lannan Foundation, the Lila Wallace – Reader's Digest
Literary Publishers Marketing Development Program,
and the Rochester Area Foundation.

Cover Design: Daphne Poulin
Typesetting: R. Foerster, York Beach, ME
Manufacturing: McNaughton & Gunn, Lithographers
BOA Logo: Mirko

BOA Editions, Ltd.
A. Poulin, Jr., President
92 Park Avenue
Brockport, NY 14420

For my mother and father

꧁꧂

Here are your waters and your watering place.
—Robert Frost

Contents

Foreword

The people in Rick Lyon's poems are real people, not symbolic instruments of their author's literary or moral ambitions. They suffer their own imperfections, their own longings, their own small triumphs, not because they are serving grand poetic or moral purposes, but because they have been allowed to have their own truths, their own reality, a sense of themselves being alive that people alive actually have. They are often wounded, by love, alcohol, indolence, rage, and by that too ready violence which seems to be the curse of the America of our moment. They love and hate each other, stab each other, even set each other afire, but somehow, poignantly, they tend each other's truths, they, and the poems in which they are realized, pay attention to one another with a fierceness all too rare in our poetry. Like characters from Wordsworth, they live their sadnesses and ordinary joys intensely, with no self-consciousness of being within a poem.

The gentrifying town Lyon's people live in — his laboratory, his picture gallery — is changing out from under them: their boats and houses rot and fall apart, they fall apart themselves, try to hang onto what they have, what they remember once having; they become ill, and die, and still they shed a special grace, tendered by the gentle sympathies of their poet. Lyon dignifies and enhances the community which he has taken to himself, just as Frost did his, and Hardy his.

Nature, in these poems, has a similar feeling of truth: nature here doesn't exist for our sake, it doesn't prettily present itself as a nostalgic romanticism, as a dream of purity embodied in trees and rocks through which the poet will maunder to succor our incompleteness. It is rather the nature we really live, vast and undeniable, but close to us, sadly enduring by our permission, hurt and soiled just as we are. The land here, the river, the woods, the few patches of unused fields, are cluttered with the apparatuses of humankind, our tools and junk, the ugliness and banalities we generate. But the poems in *Bell 8* give nature more than its due; their inclusiveness, their clear-sightedness, evoke as well as the weariness of our shortcomings, a joy in our probing consciousness, in the beauty which, despite all, the song of our language can redeem from what is beyond us. Listen to "Pile Driver":

> From the harbor now there's that old sound,
> that jangling thump as new spiles go down,
> down into the river mud.
> It drifts a little in the breeze,
> shifting closer, drifting off,
> stops, starts up again.
> The pounding getting the thing done,
> making a kind of music, meanwhile,
> the way the birds do, getting their own things done,
> and the blossoms do, pink ones, white ones, silently.
> It comes across so clearly,
> the way the heart pounds and pounds for as long as it does,
> or a bird sometimes sings out so sharply against the rest,
> that it seems it will always be like this,
> the birds, the blossoms, the beginning again.

What a lovely poem. What an apt "poetica" for this lovely book. Lyon has a delicate sense of the cadences of language, and a firm control of his own voice. It is a voice both supple and concrete, meditative and experientially insistent. It is sometimes funny ("Chasing the Muskrat") but always has a keen appreciation for the faltering rhythms of the potentially tragic:

> I guess your brain's like one of those collapsed barns you'll see
>   sometimes from the highway upstate,
> though yours still works well enough and keeps you going...

It has just as strong a sense of pure lyrical exuberance, of language sinuously gliding through its perceptions and imaginations:

> To our weekend sailors, bell 8 means home from the sea,
> that dim clang, the red buoy ahead, and the long stone arms of the
>   breakwater next,

marked at night by its green-and-white outer light and the light
    house on shore,
our river rife with shoals and shifting sand bars.

When Lyon turns, in his poems of lost love and love, to himself, he contemplates the anguish he feels, and that which somehow survives and transfigures that anguish, with as intense a regard, with as insistent a compassion; a compassion which never becomes self-pity, and never, ever, self-dramatization.

The way she'd slowly opened the door,
I should've known she was springing a trap...
I'd been foolishly pursuing the little redhead...

A sad soul, sometimes, but a good soul, modest and generous, has written this book, and sensitively inhabits it. Lyon's gift is generous, too, and there is nothing modest about it: his singing is subtle and ample, his vision sharp and large, his poems gratifying and unique.

—C. K. Williams

Burning the Meadows

You know these flames the way you know a face,
and that's the surprise now,
not the flames, not the face, but the reappearance.
There's fire on the meadows at the far end of the night,
so far that the flames seem like a memory,
like something further back, flaring up again,
some winter night, some fall night,
beyond cove and marsh, in another wind.
And then the waves of flame are through.

Maybe there's something wrong with us, some small thing,
which might surge up like fire,
leaving next to nothing of the life that was—
a cleansing fire, sometimes.
Maybe there's something we can do to keep it from happening,
something we can do once it does.
Maybe there's nothing we can do.
With us, I mean, my friend,
of whom you'd always warned me.

One Other Thing

All week, they've dredged the river,
hauling up muck from the channel.
Around the clock, the clamshell feeds
till the barge is full and dumped and back for more.
Out there in the cold dark off town, the engine churns,
the universe spins, and we sleep.

It's steadying, almost, to know that the work goes on,
the crane clanking, the cable coiling and uncoiling,
the dredge on its slow way downstream.
But it's bothersome, too.
Soon, they'll give the river back—
its long silence, the wavering mirror—
back to processions of floes,
to tankers and tugs and the wind.

It's wrong of me to want something so much,
anything but steadiness.
To move ceaselessly like the river is best—
its own mass, its own motion.
A man sick with love's torn from himself
like sand from the north.

Stone Fence Post

It's hard to hate the bulldozer,
though you almost do
because of what it's done, or been hired to do.
The old sheds, the one creeping up the hillside, the apple trees,
the big black walnut with a building built around it
because it was easier to do than to bring the thing down—
old Otto's crazy array and sloping backyard,
all brought down to this, grassless,
a dirt grade with a leaching field in it.
A new beginning, like an old man's, elsewhere.
A new beginning, then,
for someone with less shambling purposes,
the way the one shed simply went up the hillside
because it had to, eventually.
Then needing a new roof, with a new pitch to it,
one thing following another.
And all but endlessly
because old Otto's quarter century's going under.
The bright pine frame of a new addition going up
juts off the house, white,
its hemlocks, its hundred-year-old maple
with a stone fence post jammed in its base,
the way the grey ice wagon seemed jammed where it sat,
and everything else.
Old Otto took what he could.
Books, antiques, buggy wheels,

all the hand-forged iron, horses' harnesses,
tradesmen's tools of sometimes uncertain trades,
stained glass, the strange paraphernalia of other eras,
picture frames, things loved once, or never loved.
And Otto went.
Otto and his wife went back where they came from,
unlike so much that's come so far.
Unlike anything ever really does,
especially us.

Plain as Day

I got a letter once,
more or less meant to change my life.
The woman—it was a woman—did her best,
but all that ever sank in was how she'd ended.
The affair, a minor tragedy, as affairs go,
lasted some months more, with never another letter,
never another signature to say *I care.*
The words meant nothing, but had a kind of beauty,
the way a cloud does, shifting, slowly changing shape.
It was a tragedy, I said, if tragedy's caring too late.

The boy, the boy in the story,
became a man at the crossroads—
and this, much later—
where the tight circles of private lives break.
There's the road back, and the other,
the road of wonder, the only road.

Then there were many names and places,
plants and animals, too, and much dust,
cities and nations, that never really were before.
And all because of a word,
a verb, its pronoun irretrievably lost,
or transformed, married to the word itself,

the word married to the world.
Celia, her name was—"heavenly,"
but terribly of the earth.

❦

Pile Driver

From the harbor now there's that old sound,
that jangling thump as new spiles go down,
down into the river mud.
It drifts a little in the breeze,
shifting closer, drifting off,
stops, starts up again.
The pounding getting the thing done,
making a kind of music, meanwhile,
the way the birds do, getting their own things done,
and the blossoms do, pink ones, white ones, silently.
It comes across so clearly,
the way the heart pounds and pounds for as long as it does,
or a bird sometimes sings out so sharply against the rest,
that it seems it will always be like this,
the birds, the blossoms, the beginning again.

The Light on the River

I look for the light on the river, sometimes,
when I'm wanting to see something, anything, there in the dark.
And it's there, blinking on, blinking off.
It's always there, when nothing much else is,
nothing much else but myself and the light.
So I look up from a book, look the long way north, and wait—
each fourth second, marked.

There's the rumble, sometimes, of tankers and tugs
making their way, slowly, steadily, to and from the flash.
But, mostly, there's silence.
There's night, whatever the season, the light,
the all but indistinguishable river, myself.

I think these things, knowing she's gone.
Her husband inconsolable.
If there's any strength in us, ever, it must be like this—
one soul speaking to another, somewhere.

Gulls

The fish get the bugs and the birds get the fish
and nobody gets the birds because there's a law against it.
The gulls act almost as if they know that.
This one, perched on a piling,
preening, then drawing back up,
the fine white breast thrown out with each breath.
The other, afloat in the narrow channel there,
watching the silver twirling the speared fish makes,
taking another peck out of the living thing.
They eat their fill.
The green grasses and flotsam floating down from the cove as it
    empties,
then what the sea shoves back,
the way summer's shoved back now, the green tide,
the bloody fish on the dock the gull dropped,
the ancient river, alive again,
various with birds and fish, with boats,
the surrounding human, all the activity as strange, still,
as the gulls' cold cry, from high in the air,
the way human love's strange, those cries,
coming from further off, almost, than any of this,
the beginning and end, knotted together, in one instant.

The Discipline

It's not easy, watching someone's dreams die.
Little by little, the life goes—
the wife, the house, a swatch of indifferent ocean.
Love's nothing but a name for what's taken away,
little by little, but taken.
Sometimes we can blame our own foolishness, friend, for the loss,
because we've wandered down along the long rocks,
stood on the spot where those sick enough, stupid enough,
have made their dare, lost,
vanished with one surge of the sea.
Our powerlessness moves me.
How the man's stripped bit by bit, sometimes,
beaten, accepting this,
still standing until he can stand no more, and drops.
That's our strength, then, losing.

Buttercups

Getting older, you get over things quicker.
Maybe it's just because there's more to get over,
always more, so you do.
You had better, you could say, just to keep up.
Pretty soon, you're wondering what the problem was,
wondering less and less.
It's a lot like watching the seasons have their way with the pasture.
Nothing much but rock and mud for a good long while,
then the guaranteed green, the horses,
and some morning, this morning, it's all awash with yellow flowers.
That's what breaks your heart now.
They'll bury the old horse tomorrow,
and lots else, elsewhere.
You're a little amazed you're still here, really, and that's good.
That's what you think about, some nights, if you're lucky—
that you're just there, like those flowers,
and just there's good enough.

The Fire

It's an old hurt, one you hardly recognize anymore,
and it comes over you
like bad weather moving in from the north,
but you don't know what to expect.
You remember the rain, the spring rain,
and how it seemed it would never stop, but did.
First love, and like no other.
You can hardly remember what it was—
a story with a beginning, middle, and end,
though you're not sure if you've arrived at the end yet.
It's a story, part of the larger story your life is,
something you'd relate to friends, even casually,
because it's a story with a beginning, a middle,
and, for the time being, an end.
You'd relate how the woman happened into your life
and where this took you—the house on the hill, the trees,
the time of year, autumn.
More and more, in the telling, it sounds like a story,
especially to you, something which could've happened to anyone.
The woman's reddish-blond hair in the firelight,
waves of hair like firelight,
her green eyes as you looked into them, if you looked into them,
flecked with firelight, like flecks of the future,
a future you wouldn't have cared to know of.
It's the same fire, its heat, its light,

and the going out, you feel, have always felt.
It's like the end of a story,
the way the story ends and we put down the book—
the house on the hill's gone, though it lingers awhile,
like an ember, there in the fire, gone out now,
like the woman, gone now,
and you almost want to say goodbye, again,
to all of it, to everything once so full of life
for you only, for you only.
But you don't. Instead, you free it,
each and every thing, since this is different,
since you've never been able to do this before,
to bless this life and leave it behind.

The Point

The town has changed,
though spring's improving the least likely of places.
It's mainly stuck fast in old uses,
like the draggers, with women's names, along the dock,
the red-brick heap of a factory, still operating,
and the granite-rimmed point on the ocean,
sea-walled, block by block, with an apron of boulders,
so the squat half acre stays.
The gravel's churned under the cars, pulling up, pulling out,
come to take in the view of the surrounding waters,
and just as it was, years back, with her.
One night, after we'd quarreled,
she'd struck off for home in the rain
and got as far as the reed-lined causeway
before I caught her, cursing and crying,
shivering in her wet rabbit coat.
I'd shaken her by the shoulders and said *I love you,*
which triggered an embrace—
she'd calmed down in the firelight—
though I was always drunk, and there'd be no peace.

Roads

The main road's the same one called by another name—
in Essex, it's the Saybrook road, in Saybrook the Essex road—
it's what you're oriented towards.
When they changed the route number, we learned the new one,
    slowly.
Tonight there's nothing to learn.
The moist air's so heavy it sags over the waterfront,
cloud-like, refusing to rain.
All the boats, docks, buildings, and trees make a dark ground now
where the fog-haloed lights and their long reflections across the water
hold us, our arguments and griefs,
in a mild forgetful August mist,
and then the hard rain finds us.

The Roses

You might not know what's going to come along,
what will go,
but that this is the way the world works is clear.
The coral-colored roses which climb the neighbors' split-rail fence
mark the start of the summer, year after year,
and fade, and fall.
They'll take us by surprise, some morning,
arriving in full bloom, and it won't be long.
Just one last time, though,
when her brother's so sick
and their marriage has plainly failed.
But I'm thinking especially of women as beautiful as those roses,
average ones, who've come and gone,
and how often the simplest life's graced
by a strong, uncomplicated beauty,
and loved.

❦

Not Far from the City

It's the way you've clung to an old love—
always recalling her, whom you lost.
If only you could see things in themselves,
like the rock and dirt where a warehouse will go,
along a road on which a few small houses stand
and a brook cuts underneath.
It's nothing to you—
a place where people live and work,
all farmland once, but nothing to you.
The trailer park and old farmhouses on the main road,
the truck stop and apple orchards, nothing,
because you were never a part of it.
And there's no love in this,
as you'd learned from the winning local woman,
who was happily attached.

Marsh Grass

Where will this girl's troubles end, you wonder,
and wonder no further.
For now, the sun shines,
brightening the swamp where the parking lot ends.
It softens the place,
this banged-up backside of a warehouse trucks back up to.
Otherwise, it's us.
The girls in the front office, the kidding around,
the listening to what's bugging somebody,
the truckdrivers in and out the back door.
But mostly it's just the swamp out there,
the sky overhead, the season's slow changes.
It almost makes up for how little we know of each other,
just working together.
Because we're part of the season's passing,
the marsh grass gone to seed already,
this downy nothing which is life.

Summer

A man asleep among the flowers
is what I remember best.
They'd taken him out to a cot in the yard,
bordered with marigolds and day lilies,
the temporary sickbed in the sunshine and fresh air,
where he'd seemed far from the drone of lawn mowers,
the circling retriever's restlessness,
the world all around his awkward face-down sprawl.
She'd seemed faraway, too,
watching him, watching her brother,
another afternoon on the darkened porch
as he slept in a chair.
And that's what it was—
the steady, undistracted, undeceived gaze—
the equal, the answering thing,
his dying, her love.

❧

Bob's Boat

Bob's boat's one of a kind,
half house, half boat, but mostly Bob
and mostly a mess.
But look past the oddity of it,
the snow shovel stowed by the side door,
old boarding ladders along the foredeck,
look back to a time of particular care,
the charred hull, transformed.
You'd see it best in the engines, twin diesels,
two buses' worth, if rarely used,
the mahogany console in the pilothouse,
the instrument panel's silver plaque
saying *Springtime,* and it was.
The clapboard-sided superstructure's mostly windows,
because looking out's what keeps you sane,
the double-planked hull of Honduras mahogany, afloat.
Built for wartime, gutted by fire,
she'll see some other life yet.
And Bob knows. She's served him well,
through married years, and young son Bob's,
light duty of a life, a home.
Now the house plants wilt and wither
while Bob's just more oblivious,
with his bandages and ointments and sick diabetic's sores,
pharmaceutical bottles and boxes spilled around the saloon,
like the rain water, dribbling in,

and the whole heap sails on.
Our skipper, dozing off, in front of the television,
the new dog, up in his spot on the sofa,
and outside, all the lights on,
on again, on the surface of the water,
dark, cold, another year done,
but warm in here, an eternal seventy degrees,
some consolation or guarantee
against bone-chilling times, some earlier era,
if there's a reason, that is,
a reason for spring, for anything.

Stroll

Who's to blame?
Not the lay of the land, which is to say, the woman—
she's simply there.
In the morning, with the birds singing,
with the sun breaking through so many trees,
there's no one to blame.
It might be, she's like a season,
like spring, or autumn,
and calls us like this.
There won't be a road anywhere in all of it,
but small flowers lost in the grass,
in the dying grass, catching our eyes,
bright specks like memories are,
and she's part of this,
but we weren't going anywhere anyway.

Caroline

We'd found bats in your airy, tree-shaded house,
and learned there's little to be done about the mostly harmless
    transients,
except to locate and block their natural entry.
Drifting off in the current of a mild summer night,
you'd leaned on the sofa back, gazing into the foyer behind us,
then peered—your lips drawn into a smile—
and faintly asked, *What's that? Is that a bat?*
Oh my God, it's a bat, you sighed, hiding your face in the cushion,
while the homing creature swooped on us, turned tail, and went
    upstairs.
Your curly mane might somehow have ensnared a bat,
but you'd not cared to witness our guest's circular flight in your
    bedroom, anyway.
He swiftly dodged all my broom-swats and jabs
till a combination punch sent him rocketing out through the open
    porch door,
which he hadn't a chance to find by himself.
Our waylaid evening more nearly resembled our romance, not easy,
when, curious, I opened the attic door on two more bats,
and we had no choice but to let them be.

Goodbye, Randy Brown

You'd brought back a roulette ashtray, stamped *Fabulous Las Vegas,*
and told how you and Gladys had bumped into Ralph,
who was sitting on a park bench, eating an ice cream cone.
That was a story to match one of Ralph's own,
like the time he stopped in some Texas town
and left with a waitress and a pair of lizard skin boots.
He's still got the boots, and we've got him.
You must've used your narrow-eyed stare to make him grin,
but I can't remember if either of you won anything else.
When I try the roulette wheel, it comes up *black 2*—
we'll bury you tomorrow, May 2.
I can't help but wonder what God's plan is—
you should've been a minister, with your deacon grandfather, for your
    mother—
but you'd always helped us to wonder less, to trust more.
Randy Brown, man of few words,
whose life was brief, whose death was swift,
you taught us, what the boys in the Monkey Farm bar might learn,
that a lost soul is only lost.
You'd known times when the joke was on you,
like your return trip to the package store, after the car crash,
with the neck and cap of the smashed jug—seal intact—to obtain a
    replacement.
The five years in which you'd done nothing so silly
might've turned into ten, twenty, or thirty.
Over coffee once, we'd laughed so hard we were crying.

You'd told one funny hunting story after another,
starting with the one about your dad's dog, Ragmop, who'd eat the
    animals
till the day a squirrel jumped up and got him by the balls.
The doctors found morphine wouldn't kill your cancer pain,
so God did.
Tomorrow, Donnelley's will shut down the presses for two hours,
and Frank says they might as well.
I'll be going home soon, you'd told Eleanor,
who later realized what you meant.

❦

Almost Autumn

I don't know what's growing on it—
weeds and a bush of yellow flowers that must be tickseed sunflowers
    or something like them—
whatever landed on the rotting paint float and liked it there.
I see such stuff is done on purpose in the Orient and called floating
    islands
but Bob just let the thing rot to the point it was tending in that
    direction—
some moss and grass, last year, and now a few feet's worth of
    whatever's at work.
Almost autumn is what it all means.
The bees living in a neighboring piling are making the rounds,
the biggest nets the spiders have left catch the morning dew,
everything straining, stretching,
more than aware of what's to be done at summer's end,
in the diminishing hours of daylight and cooler nights,
foraging for the last scraps of food to be found.

Jimmy

He'd always have a bag of bread for the ducks and swans,
which eventually made a point of paying a visit,
gangs of them, once their babies had hatched.
Feeding the ducks helped to pass the time
between shuttling people back and forth on the ferry—
boring work, but he was out on the water with the ducks and boats
    and little to bother him,
and the job was hardly more tedious than managing a gas station,
    which he did, weekends.
Living with his parents, mid-thirties, a boxer once,
he wasn't going anywhere, but wasn't a problem, anyway.
Then his dad died and he started talking a little crazy—
the death, drug use, maybe both—
quit the job, and was soon dodging the cops.
You'd wonder whether someone might half wish insanity on himself,
    to make it real,
acting crazy and evil as if to eliminate all doubt,
because, next thing, at knife point, he'd tried to drag a girl into the
    woods,
she'd broken free, and he's now found a new home for a long while.
His story's less grim than what happened last winter
when a trooper walked up to a van, beside the highway,

two minutes too late to save the woman.
But the ugly things won't prove less so.
The swans move as if nothing can harm them,
turning away, proud, and not to be touched.

❧

Ace

As he stood near the door of the docked boat,
his tanned neck caught the dim yellow light—
provoked, drunk, he'd try to get even with me
because I'd collared him once,
so I watched the dark figure carefully.
Belligerent as he was, he was too weak to fight.
The booze had ruined him.
His wife, job, driver's license, all gone.
He lived, at forty, with his mother
and would visit a friend on the island where I ran the launch.
The friend lived on a boat and preferred his company to none,
letting him lounge there, alone, if he wasn't drinking.
This time, he'd got loaded, though,
returning gingerly down the steep dock ramp—
I pressed him about his bagged bottle, two-thirds drained,
and he'd ridiculously rolled up his shirtsleeves.
In one unconscious instant—he'd come at me—
I'd pinned him to the rail, with a forearm across his throat.
The news of his black-and-blue shiner, later, was trouble enough.
Next thing, he tried suicide, after the old man called his bluff,
rolling his car, one night, and stabbing himself in the gut.
Nothing changed. He returned from the hospital,
an overlooked case, acting cockier than ever.
I couldn't fathom his tolerant friend, looking out for the guy—

on the mother's behalf, he explained
and added, *he's not long for this world*
from which the wise one's now gone.

꙳

Franklin

The young guys on the work crew couldn't follow the lunch-break
    conversation,
the way he'd spoken of the old town dump, just closed down, as if it
    were prime real estate.
No one can touch the land for fifty years, the law runs.
The kids came from other towns, though, and hadn't hauled loads to
    the place—
the man-made dome that's now reached its full height,
where gulls once scrambled above the bulldozed earth
and the long river flares out into the ocean.
He'd lost the foreman's job, finally, and then got hospitalized—
the doctor told him, keep it up, he wouldn't last another year—
so he stayed straight awhile.
He wouldn't live to see forty.
Now the place with the panoramic view is somewhere you wouldn't
    be bothered,
somewhere the cops, who knew him well, wouldn't turn up,
which is what he'd have wanted, drinking and drugging again.
We'd all laughed at his stories of Nam
and were mostly fooled by his tough talk.
Two local kids found him lying on a mattress,
faceup, naked, in the rain.

Confession

I've lain, Lord, in my own vomit and shit,
three times I can recall, and I don't care to awaken that way again,
unless illness, unless dying demands it.
What I've done, young, drunk, self-fouled, makes no confession,
not when, all the more clear, there were witnesses.
Nothing to confess.
And what could I tell you, blackest of hearts,
friend, lover, enemy, that you don't already know?
You're an open book, a story, the names of whose characters have all
        been changed.
You've nothing to hide, no lies that won't be untold,
you, Lord, heart, a furnace of sunlight
where there are no shadows,
and the cold metal that forms there, like thought, your soul,
is the one version of truth you might own, so take it.

Major Scott

His group of Twentieth Air Force brass had planned the A-bomb
    missions.
Twenty-five years later, his marriage falling apart,
he'd turn up at my parents' house, raging, crying, claiming the FBI
    was after him,
frightening my mother, brother, and me with his crazy talk and fury,
calmed only by my father, who'd fought the Japanese too.
Then the drunken delirious nights ended.
He moved south to St. Thomas and soon died of a heart attack.
We'd vacationed there once, while he was away,
staying at his hilltop apartment overlooking the bay,
and for a long time afterwards I thought he'd died a suicide—
as if the man's madness, like the fierce beauty of the place, would all
    end there, wrenchingly,
where the flamboyant trees' flame-like flowers won't stop burning.

The Broom

My father told me the story when I was older,
when I wasn't so much at odds with him,
though I can remember no occasion, no reason, for the story,
other than his being in a meditative mood.
During a party, he'd poked my grandfather, in fun, with a fireplace
    broom,
and was shoved violently against a wall.
My grandfather apologized by relating an incident from his past—by
    blaming the broom, really.
In Central America, he'd once witnessed a brawl in a barroom,
where one man had taunted another, with a broom,
and whose stomach, in return, had been slashed with a machete.
While someone went for a doctor, my grandfather held his guts from
    falling out.
Whether he lived or died wasn't a part of my father's story.

Flocks

The crane comes up with another yard of black muck,
timbers dangling, caught in the clamshell bucket's iron grip,
twirling slightly, up high, then dumped,
cables snapping and thwacking along the steel boom.
A new bulkhead's going in,
the monochromatic tones of the diesel, straining, slackening,
as the crane slats back and forth.
In motion, too, dead brown leaves of autumn,
pressed flat to the water, pinned to the outbound tide.
Fewer and fewer fish now—
the big schools of bunker, chased in by hungry blues,
flying clear of the surface sometimes, fins abuzz,
the less lucky ones, in their whirling sidewise dying.
The season points south.
Loose flocks of geese, trailing off,
a dense dark wash of swallows, wing to wing, in the evening.
Now, though, up above the quieter waterfront, an osprey drifts, and
  drops.
Headfirst, wings crumpled back—with a splash, it's in—
lifting up and off again, talons clutching the silver-sided cargo,
the doomed fish, lifting it higher,
carrying it higher and away.

The Woods

Maybe old Lois had left without a trace—
her house, the one you loved, would still be there—
so I stopped and checked, after years of avoiding the place, the distant
    town,
and saw the name on the mailbox had changed.
A car pulled into the driveway,
waiting while I backed out of the way,
and then sped past—the reddish-blond hair, the face, yours.
I'd left in a panic
and come back, in the dark, to find no one home.
The strange story would have ended there,
but I called the next day.
You told me how Lois had died,
you'd married—I knew—
and built another house further in the woods, hidden from view.
So I thanked you again—
the old lost love who changed my life—
happy for you and your longed-for family.
The bright dust of that evening in June,
the surrounding trees in their early green,
must've been streaked by one last ray from the sun, then,
the way the matter of our lives flares up in us, sometimes,
with love, remorse, those fires the dust knows nothing of.

Angels

We couldn't tell where the singing was coming from,
though the priest had introduced the music as Donna's favorite song,
an easily identifiable popular one.
Then we spotted the girl, to the right of the front pew,
catching her blond head and shoulders, just above those seated,
as she clung to the slippery ladder of the tune.
Eleanor'd given her a hug, after,
while the rest was harder—the sudden coming together—
till the last long walk out of church.
Donna's husband, mother, father, and four brothers,
all followed where the casket led.
The afternoon's light snow left no trace.
In the parking lot, we'd spoken quietly of Eleanor's grief
and found some insignificant subject to amuse ourselves with,
but now Randy's ominously ill and the cornered one.
You light up my life, the girl sang,
and her careful singing had strangely removed all doubt
that we might live powerfully beyond the grave.

Joey

I guess your brain's like one of those collapsed barns you'll see
    sometimes from the highway upstate,
though yours still works well enough and keeps you going.
I want to ask Bart for all the details of what happened then, what I
    hadn't known till now,
but he doesn't answer my calls.
He must've taken the family on their end-of-the-summer vacation
    somewhere,
while the state's so green and wildflower-filled.
It's where we'd all grown up and suffered at the hands of the big guys.
Neary and Gilman, you'd smile and slug us in the chest.
You and Steve jumped out of a plane together once,
and you'd ended up in the Airborne.
Steve cried in private at the hospital, until he could look at you, after
    you shot yourself in the head.
They'd cut away part of the skull to ease the swelling.
Most of us have once wanted to do the same—
to put a bullet in the brain to kill the pain.
Nobody'd dared but you, and you'd lived.
Maybe your twenty-five years' pain blinded you—the fatherless
    childhood and failed love—
because you wouldn't have wanted us to see you like this,
wheelchair-bound and a burden.

In your shame, you're bound to our conscience now,
like the fire on a distant beach, which anchors the night,
and speaks to us who've once been saved.

King's Cross

I'd walked a long way, looking for a convenience store
where I could buy a late-night cup of coffee to go—
to take away, as the English say—
so I asked a woman walking alongside me
whether I might find one in the neighborhood ahead.
Yes, she said, and added *Would you like business?*
I didn't understand what she'd said, at first, so she repeated it.
Once I understood and declined the offer,
she'd given the directions to me, anyway.
Maybe she overheard me muttering the strange word as I crossed the
    street.
She got in line behind me at the storefront food stand
where the pieces of barbecued chicken were on display—
fidgeting and biting her nails then.
The vendor'd become agitated on seeing her
and tossed my change back.
Her curly blond hair fell over her dark green coat.
Maybe I wasn't unlucky last night, after all,
with the redheaded Belgian professor Anne,
whom I'd propositioned unsuccessfully,
kissed goodnight, and missed.

The Friend

Maybe the same two white cabbage butterflies as yesterday
flirt near the fence today,
where the breaking wave of a rose bush rolls over it.
So many roses, like kisses, must make the bugs giddy,
tumbling toward the doorway I'm looking out of
above the yellow-flowered Katherine Dykes.
White on white, they dance their dance and go.
Maybe it's a lovers' quarrel, though—
a cheerful scene, anyway.
My neighbor's girlfriend's been looking for something like this—
man by man, country by country—
a pretty prospect, a gay afternoon before the long night.

ఞ

Lost

I was looking for your cross, lady—
the tall stone one my friend said was out here somewhere—
so I followed the long road around and came back where I'd started.
The roads had forked. I was certainly lost.
When I set off again, in the wrong direction, I spotted the stubby
    brown cross anyway.
There it was, among the pines, like a figure seen from behind.
And there, too, was the nearby house I'd taken my bearings from.
Your woods, Katrina, are too small to get lost in.
The sun set behind your snow-covered grave
and I turned to face the way you do—east.

❧

Steffi's New Paintings

She's removed so much from her paintings now,
there's nothing left but a color, a line.
Their problems are simple but can't easily be solved.
The stubborn paintings won't budge.
So she's started putting things back in—
dresses from her childhood, palm fronds,
telephones, staircases,
images from old Japanese poems she's read at lunchtime,
falling leaves, magpies and flowers—daisies are nice—
things remembered from long ago, just seen,
and maybe never seen till now.
Sometimes it's all so tiring she has to lie down and rest.
Her first wild collage-like painting came easily
but she's afraid it won't happen again—
the tropical profusion of color making the heart pound.
Still, she keeps putting things in—
dogs, hands, more dresses,
a trail of footprints in the snow.

Winterbloom

The frizzy yellow flower on a bare branch,
which blooms so late in the year when nothing else is blooming,
is witch hazel, and said to cure a broken heart.
The showy midwinter flowers get our attention, anyway,
and maybe the stringy blossoms on their wand-like branch are
      magical.
But the flowers, birds, and trees mean nothing at all to me, dear heart,
unless they mean something to you,
whose animal-like presence is always just out of sight, in the woods,
watching me with sharp eyes.
The wood spirit, the wind spirit, in the pines outside my window
says we love what we love
because it summons us to each other
who'll be no more before long.

Chasing the Muskrat

Molly, who's missing her two front teeth,
shows me how she can step from one stone to another
near the water's edge where she and her sister Kate are playing.
I'm perched on the guard rail along the street, just above their heads,
ready to leap to the rescue if anyone slips on the slippery stones
but nobody does.
Next thing, out in the dark still water, twenty feet off,
up pops the muskrat I've just told the girls about—
how he looked like a cat and swam like a rat—
because I'd seen him that morning.
So the girls holler and chase him along the waterfront docks
as he swims past the fleet of boats moored there,
spotting our quarry, who'll sometimes dive and resurface—where?—
who finally turns and leads us back where we'd come from.
He disappears into the rock pile—goodbye, muskrat—
and might've just been looking for some attention, anyway,
on this chilly evening in April, with nothing much to do,
just poking around down along the waterfront, the way we like to.

Cat and Mouse

The way she'd slowly opened the door,
I should've known she was springing a trap.
Her new boyfriend, whom I'd heard nothing about, was standing in
    the living room.
I'd been foolishly pursuing the little redhead
and was picking her up for what I thought was a date.
We'd finally get matters set straight.
She'd let me down badly in the past and I'd criticized her for it.
Maybe the trap was her revenge.
Maybe the immature woman failed to notice the damage she'd done.
She kissed the guy goodbye as if I wasn't in the room at all
and said she was puzzled when I told her later I wouldn't be back.
Driving down Main Street, one night,
I turned the corner as a cat slowly followed a mouse across the road.
They'd paused, briefly, and continued along once I'd stopped too.
So formal, the agony.
Tonight two swans glide by, almost invisible in the dark.
The birds have mated for life.
What's lost washes over me
as featureless as the wind riffling the dry grasses of the marsh.

Hattie Downing's Bequest

She had a will alright, the old dowager lady
whose house hovered on its hillock above our town,
not visible from the main road,
and not visible from anywhere now—the house, that is—
because she wasn't about to let the developers get it.
Her friends knew she'd have the place torn down when she died,
the three-story house, the barns, and the children's playhouse—
the whole estate's been plucked from its gently sloping lawn,
bulldozed and burned, to make a park.
She'd have missed all our valuable local meadows and fields, now lost,
and wanted us to keep one town park's worth of grass and trees, hers.
It must have helped focus her last years,
thinking of those to-be flames, which weren't to harm the trees,
while she drove her longtime chauffeur around, finally, all the roles
        reversed,
till he **was** gone, and then her—
the fiery one, whose home is Downing park.

K. T. Delios

We should've figured someone with such exquisite tastes, a buyer and
    seller of fine antiques, was rotten to the core—
what's taste, anyway, but another futile statement about yourself?
We had clues, and now he's proven himself no good,
beaten his estranged wife to within an inch of her life,
and been arrested, as reported in the local paper.
She'd had taste, too, owning a high-class dress shop,
but had left town, sensibly.
You'd think he'd've done likewise but—no—he's moved into her old
    place—
all the duck decoys, statuary, highboys and oriental rugs.
Stupidity's expensive.
I've seen it firsthand, operating my little ferryboat,
transporting the mostly human cargo from island to mainland.
The partygoers on their yachts come and go, all summer,
while the townsfolk stay put.
If the boaters head into town for the evening, they usually come back
    sober and polite,
but the local off-season crowd's a rowdy one.
It's anyone's guess how the rowdies will come back—
one couple, last fall, came back bickering and murderous.
I'd been unable to read the guy, tight-lipped with a thin mustache,
but within minutes after I'd dropped them off, he was pummeling his
    companion,
a tough-talking blonde who'd seen better days.
A kid distracted the guy,

so the woman could run back to their boat, *Good Times,*
and then let the guy have it—
four times in the leg, with a kitchen knife.
The cops and the ambulance crew came and went—
plus some sobbing friends of the couple—
while the onlookers tried to put together a story that made sense.
Next day, the guy'd come back, bandaged, and left.
The woman spent the night in jail, no doubt,
after the wife-beater, shoeless and shivering, was ferried across on his
     stretcher to the hospital.
It's so close—the depravity—
you can reach out to touch the cold, trembling body.
Strolling past the antiques man's soon-to-be-former place one evening
I noticed a hand exerciser near a pile of paperwork by the window seat
     in the shop,
and pictured him there, calmly testing his grip.

Burns

Everyone thought it was shocking but awfully funny
when they heard how the guy's wife doused him with paint thinner
    and lit a match.
Donations for Gary Morgan, the Chef Flambé, the sign said,
over the bucket at the local bar restaurant where he'd worked.
He survived, badly burned, and his wife June got carted off to the state
    women's prison,
claiming the fire was an accident, but her story didn't ring true.
He'd burst into flames while they were in bed anyway.
It wasn't funny but unlikely.
I suppose there's nothing quite so frightening as getting burned alive,
while the flames lick away your flesh, and you suffocate, if that's what
    happens.
It's over quickly.
Maybe having to live, tormented, with some kinds of knowledge is worse,
but most of the meanest criminals aren't.
We're left wondering whether there's anything amiss with our own
    conscience,
which is all we've got, it seems,
and our sense of humor, supremely important,
and thank God it wasn't your wife who lit the match, friend,
although it might well have been, given a more sinister twist to our
    mostly inelegant lives.
Gary's coming home soon and June isn't.

Night Heron

I can't say as I've seen it, the night heron,
though I caught it by surprise once, down on the dock in the dark.
Not the most attractive creature, as I recall.
It's just a shadowy shape on the far dock, across the creek the ferry
    crosses,
where the bird waits, head sunk in its ruffled feathers,
watching for the fish I've never seen it catch.
It's done well, I'd say,
judging from the large white splotches of birdshit
which have blossomed on the dock, come morning.
The dark shape flies off if someone approaches
but the passing cars and their headlights don't bother it.
I suppose the yellow dock lights attract fish and give the bird a
    convenient place to work,
which is all it's about, I guess—
the lonely bird, the work.

Bell 8

To our weekend sailors, bell 8 means *home from the sea,*
that dim clang, the red buoy ahead, and the long stone arms of the
    breakwater next,
marked at night by its green-and-white outer light and the lighthouse
    on shore,
our river rife with shoals and shifting sand bars.
Home's around the westerly bend, past the iron railroad bridge and
    under the highway's plain highflying one,
a small peninsular town, wedged between coves,
whose Main Street ends at the water.
The old wharf the archaeologist dug up has been covered over again—
he got what he wanted—
while out in the harbor, off the waterfront park,
the crew on the little green barge drops another season's moorings.
The clothing shop at the head of the street has been dismantled.
Its plate glass windows stand empty—
at night now, they're jet-black.
Twenty years ago, the storefront housed a pharmacy,
and then a cafe, which got closed when an ill-disposed newcomer
    bought the block—
to avenge a slight, supposedly—
which cost the locals their convenient breakfast and lunch.
The hardware store's gone, too, displaced by rising rents,
and our grocer's upcoming retirement might bring another clothing
    shop.
The town grows more and more exclusive,

with grander mansions, finer views, underscoring what's lost.
Old man Spring was poor but kind.
The boat he lived on, all these years, is on the bottom now.
He died, and then it sank,
though they'd have happily gone down together.
Maybe his spirit came built into the name.
Last fall, the guts of his boat conked out—
the furnace, the water pump, and even the shitter—
but he replaced everything.
Sometimes he'd take in boarders, on not-yet-broken faith.
It's what we lack, mostly.
From Main Street's tree-lined descent to the river,
the only moving thing, this morning, drives steadily past,
the bright blue tanker, which makes the river look small.

꘠

Youth

As unprepared as one might be to accept the horrible truth,
that all the rest of your life's been a kind of denouement of the main
    event,
love, a death, war—so strangely embracing both—
the thing turned away from, finally, with a sigh,
you realize your life's passed, revolved around the one moment of
    passion.
How ever attain to anything like it again?
It's impossible, of course, when nothing can match the shock of the
    first time—
the first taste, the initiation—
not even a lifetime of violence and wildness can match it.
There will be glimmers of the original fury, no more.
The way the girl sat in the library with her back turned to us,
her long blond hair rolled with a half-turn, where a bow had been,
the most beautiful thing in the world then.
Simply to have loved is beauty enough, and life enough.
On a summer morning, I visited my friend's grave for the first time,
the small hills, the blossoming trees, everything in its place,
the morning, sharper and brighter.
You set your chin, smile, and depart,
looking straight ahead now, a tear in the lower right-hand corner.

Marie

Marie, the Boston lesbian anarchist feminist poet,
who tried to seduce me near the end of my junior year of college,
was a Latina, I think, from New York, self-consciously literary, and
    ponderously so,
when everything about her was dark, like the skinny brown cigarettes
    she smoked, her long bohemian skirts,
and, later, her intentions toward me.
We had classes together, writer-like talks,
and I must've become her protégé, by accident,
lunching with her at the faculty lounge, hiding behind her mature
    presence,
while she tutored me, mostly, in art and life
and subjects like sex which I'd never discussed with anyone else.
She was ill, unattractive, and bisexual,
and I was a twenty-one-year-old virgin budding poet—
I saw later she was lonely.
In her dark, dignified way, she nearly pulled off my erotic initiation,
    though.
Maybe we stumbled into it—which is how it happens, mostly—
while she was staying, briefly, at a hotel on campus.
I went there with her once, in my unguarded way.
From the window, I pointed out the steeple of a church in the
    neighborhood where I lived,
and then she drew the curtains, sharply, on the afternoon sun.
As abruptly as she shut the curtains, she sat down on the bed and
    unzipped her boots.

She wanted me to look at her book manuscript, supposedly.
While I choked down some tasteless health-food bread and straight
     whiskey,
she rolled a fat joint, lit it, and passed it to me.
The way the tobacco bled profusely through the white cigarette paper—
the grass must've made me think this?—
I thought strangely of her menses and was feeling ill.
Then she disappeared into the bathroom for what seemed like forever,
and I could guess what was next.
By chance, I'd gotten the advice, which girls must get more than boys,
to choose wisely, the first time you go to bed with someone, because
     you'll always remember it—
and not long afterwards, after Marie, I stumbled drunkenly into bed,
making instinctive love to the woman I never forgot, not for years of
     trying.
When Marie emerged from the bathroom, I told her I had to leave,
and she gestured to me in a way, inviting and hopeless,
with her hands outstretched at her sides, as if to say *come to me,* and I
     didn't.
The next day she just glared at me.
Maybe she'd been my erotic initiation, after all.
The hundreds of ways it might've gone, had I gone to her, years ago,
are like the fuel and fire that drive so much of life, including art.

The Island

Reflected on the water, the lights are flamelike, flickering
in orange swatches where the wind ripples the moving tidal cove.
The long shapes beneath the dock's lighting are like torches
whose motions make companions in the night.
In the winter stillness, the flames flicker and burn.
For all the flowering of houses being built, the boats coming and going
    in summer,
the changes and commotion in town, our daily lives,
we'd seem misguided, mostly, but hopeful.
I hadn't noticed till now all we've lost. The seven lights in line on the
    island,
their strange friendly ceaseless flaring.

Paradise

I don't know why I think of Father Damien of Molokai
except that being so finicky and fastidious, you'd think of someone
    who wasn't.
It's what might flake off in the fires, this life burning upwards,
all the worrisome cares, falling away, and fueling the higher ones.
Take those islands heaved up from the sea volcanically,
rife with such vegetation and sun-drenched color, they're paradise,
even for those sick ones, torn from their families,
the flesh melting, going numb, nibbled by rats.
It's history, Father Damien's death in the leprosarium—
what he chose, and what chose him,
in this place, a short boat ride to the west.
She'd have gone, my mother reports,
and one other woman, but for the rest of the tour group.
So there it sat, as secure as before,
that small prong of land jutting into the Pacific,
its flowers once food for the bees
till someone said even the honey was tainted—
afloat like a soul, unburdened by ignorance or dread.

The Deer

It wasn't anyplace you'd normally see a deer,
which the deer must've known—
that big splash, not some kid fallen off the dock
but just what Ursula'd come hollering about, dogs barking,
the poor convinced thing swimming for its life
across the narrow creek, leaving the island behind.
With the marina over there, the town here, it made no sense,
but up piled boulders and through the parking lot,
she'd bounded into the small swamp.
That Saturday evening in May, with nobody going anywhere
she'd have found her way to the next cove,
and maybe, come nightfall, swum back home.
The other side of the river, being where deer come from,
was where the conversation turned then.
How somebody'd hit one, years back, and run off the road—
the way it ended with his best friend's wife dead,
the man leaving town, the wife and kids gone.
We talk for a while because it's calming, the commotion and after,
bringing you back home, hard, to who you are.

Acknowledgments

Acknowledgment is made to the editors of the following magazines in which these poems first appeared:

The Agni Review: "Buttercups" and "The Point";

The American Poetry Review: "Burning the Meadows," "One Other Thing" and "Stone Fence Post";

Embers: "The Fire";

Graham House Review: "The Broom";

Ironwood: "Plain as Day," "Pile Driver," "The Light on the River," "Gulls" and "The Discipline";

Kansas Quarterly: "Bell 8," "Bob's Boat" and "The Woods";

The Massachusetts Review: "Confession";

The Nation: "Almost Autumn" and "The Island";

North Dakota Quarterly: "Major Scott" and "Joey";

Partisan Review: "Jimmy";

The Plum Review: "Roads";

Tar River Poetry: "Paradise," "Flocks" and "The Deer."

The author would like to thank the Virginia Center for the Creative Arts and the Corporation of Yaddo for residencies and the Connecticut Commission on the Arts for a fellowship which aided in the completion of this book.

About the Author

Rick Lyon was born in San Juan, Puerto Rico, in 1953 and grew up in Halifax, Nova Scotia, and Syracuse, New York. He holds degrees from Boston and Columbia Universities and is the recipient of a fellowship from the Connecticut Commission on the Arts. His poems have been published in *The American Poetry Review, Ironwood, The Massachusetts Review, The Nation* and *Partisan Review.* He has had residencies at the Virginia Center for the Creative Arts and Yaddo. In 1989 he received the "Discovery"/*The Nation* Award. Since 1986 he has operated a ferryboat at a marina on the Connecticut River. He lives in Essex, Connecticut.

BOA EDITIONS, LTD.
NEW POETS OF AMERICA SERIES

༄